# Early Religious History of Maryland.

### MARYLAND NOT A ROMAN CATHOLIC COLONY,

Religious Toleration not an Act of Roman Catholic Legislation.

---

being

The Substance of a Lecture delivered before the Guild of "All Saints Church," Baltimore,

by the

REV. B. F. BROWN,

*And Published by Request.*

---

BALTIMORE:
INNES & CO., BOOK PRINTERS.
1876.

In the interest of creating a more extensive selection of rare historical book reprints, we have chosen to reproduce this title even though it may possibly have occasional imperfections such as missing and blurred pages, missing text, poor pictures, markings, dark backgrounds and other reproduction issues beyond our control. Because this work is culturally important, we have made it available as a part of our commitment to protecting, preserving and promoting the world's literature. Thank you for your understanding.

# Maryland Never a Roman Catholic Colony.

The perversions of history which come before us with all the assurance of truth, are both hurtful and difficult of correction. They mislead successive generations, deceiving their judgment and shaping their action. Tradition and myth form a large part of what men call history; and human selfishness, credulity, and prejudice, transmute them into the solidity of well-accredited facts.

No sphere of human thought is so prolific of such misleading as the religious history of individuals and nations. Often the opinion of many generations respecting some historical character or action is utterly away from the truth; because ignorance or prejudice has misstated the facts of the case; and most persons are content to accept the current view, without questioning its accuracy. In this way history is manufactured from falsehood or fancy, while frequent and confident repetition of the same lie will often silence the timid remonstrant, and confirm in error the doubtful questioner.

The good people of Maryland, in common with a large part of our whole nation, and thinking people everywhere, have been accustomed to receive, as an unquestionable fact, an assertion respecting the early history of Maryland, its settlement and government, which has no foundation in point of fact; yet has been used to mislead the ignorant, and silence the honest inquirer after truth. The error in question has been incorporated into our school-books, asserted in our newspapers, reiterated by politicians, in the interest of partisan discussion, and preached from pulpit and rostrum, until nearly our whole people give it credence, and regard the man who would call it in question as either wanting in knowledge, or blinded by prejudice. Every intelligent person who has passed the age of childhood has, in some form, met the statement that our good old State of Maryland was first settled by Roman Catholics, and that on her soil, under the government of a Roman Catholic Proprietor, and by the free act of a Roman Catholic Legislature, the grand principle of freedom to religious opinion and worship was first enunciated. In different forms of statement, embellished by all the arts of the rhetorician, and enforced by the cunning of the politician and the zeal of the propagandist, this dream of the imagination has been put forth as fact, to refute the charge of intolerance which all history sustains against the Roman religion, and to show that intolerance and persecution are not *essential* attributes of a government loyal to the Papacy. My present purpose is to present the facts of our colonial history, and elucidate their bearing upon this great question.

There is just enough of the semblance of truth in the popular idea of our colonial origin to make the deception of those who will not, or cannot, study the real facts in the case, complete. We propose to develop these facts, in such forms as will show that there is not the first element of truth in the claim, that a Roman Catholic Proprietor, and a Roman Catholic Legislature, of their own will and generosity, made a law giving *liberty* and *equality* to all, for the exercise of their religious opinions and worship, and protecting them in the same. This is the substance of the popular statement of the matter; otherwise it would have no force as an argument and illustration in the discussion between Romanists and Protestants; and on the question of the safety of religious liberty in our country, in the event of a Roman Catholic majority, throwing the control of the Government into their hands.

To make good the popular view relative to the policy of religious toleration which characterized Lord Baltimore's administration, it must be proven, *first*, that he had the legal right under his charter, and under the laws of England, to restrict or exclude the Protestant religion and worship, and make his own faith and church — the Roman Catholic — the sole religion of the colony. Unless Lord Baltimore had this power, both under the general laws of England and by the privileges of his charter, the whole claim of a broad and tolerant policy for Baltimore and his Catholic Legislature falls to the ground.

I assert that Lord Baltimore had no such power conferred by his charter; nor had the King of England, who gave him the charter, any right or power to vest him with such a prerogative, even had he designed to do so. Lord Baltimore did not exclude Protestants from his Maryland colony, restrict them in the exercise of their religion, nor set up a Roman Catholic establishment. He did neither one nor the other, because he had neither the right nor the power to do so. If I can make good this position, then the boasted Toleration Act proves nothing for the purpose to which it is continually alleged, and the claim appears as an unfounded assumption. No one, I presume, will question that England was, at the time, a Protestant nation, and that the Protestant religion was established by law, to the entire exclusion of the Roman worship. We are to look at the constitution and laws of England to enable us to interpret Lord Baltimore's charter correctly. Here we shall find what this charter, from an English king sworn to support the laws and institutions of the nation, gave Baltimore authority to do, and also what, under the English law, he had no authority to do.

When an English King or an English Parliament, in legal acts or language, speaks of Holy Church and of the True Christian Religion, the sense is clear, as meaning the church and religion established and protected by the law of the land. Such allusions mean neither Romanism on the one side; nor Protestant Dissent on the other. At the very time when Lord Baltimore obtained his Maryland charter, the law of England opposed, and sought to repress, both Roman and Protestant dissent; while it protected and sought to extend the faith and worship of the Established Church through all the English dominion at home and abroad. Holy Church and the True Christian Religion could not mean the Roman Catholic Church: for against it the law and government protested. The great mass of the English nation rejected the Roman religion; and so keenly alive were both Parliament and people to the memory of the Smithfield fires of the Bloody Mary and the Papal Bishops, that they sought to guard against the recurrence of such a danger, by a rigorous exclusion of all Roman clergy from the kingdom of England. The English people had not forgotten that only seventy-three years before, Pope Paul the Fourth forbade Elizabeth to ascend the throne of England until she submitted her pretensions to him, and declared England to be a fief of the Apostolic See. They still remembered that Pius the Fifth, eleven years later, issued a bull against Elizabeth when she had been eleven years England's glorious Queen, declaring her a "pretended Queen of England," absolving all her subjects from allegiance to her, and cursing all who adhered to her as excommunicate heretics. Only fifty years before, the "invincible" Armada of Spain, with the blessing of the Pope, hovered around the shores of England, commissioned by the *Pastor Pastorum* to convert by the gentle appliances of rack and stake the heretic English to the true faith, and win them back to the loving embrace of the Holy Father. Only thirty years before, the Gunpowder Plot sought to destroy the government by blowing up King, Lords and Commons, when assembled in Parliament. These events all conspired to beget in the English nation such an intense hatred to Roman Catholicism, as dangerous to the peace and liberty of the realm, that Parliament, under Elizabeth and James, passed severe repressive laws against the public exercise of the Roman Catholic religion, forbade the entrance of Romish priests within the kingdom, and compelled the English Romanist to attend the public worship of the English Church, under the penalty of twenty pounds per month. Such was the state of the public mind of the nation, and such were the laws of England, at the time Lord Baltimore obtained his charter for the territory of Maryland from King Charles. We mention these things not to approve them, but as showing the state of the English mind, and the laws of the realm, relative to the Roman Catholic Church; and as proving beyond question our assertion, that under the English law, and by the terms of his charter, Lord Baltimore had neither right nor power to restrict the full liberty of the Protestant faith and worship of the realm of England, or to set up a Roman Catholic establishment, as the religion of his colony.

We will now review the terms of the charter, and see how they accord with the position we have taken. The terms Catholic or Protestant do not occur in the charter; nor anything equivalent to the narrower and more technical sense in which they are commonly used. But there are terms in the charter which, interpreted as they must be, in the sense of the constitution and laws of the realm, put the legal meaning of the charter, in all that pertains to ecclesiastical matters, beyond question. The fourth section of the charter provided that —

"the patronages and advowsons of all churches which (with the increasing worship and religion of Christ) within the said region, islands, islets and limits aforesaid hereafter shall happen to be built; together with license and faculty of erecting and founding churches, chapels and places of worship in convenient and suitable places within the premises, and of causing the same to be dedicated and consecrated according to the ecclesiastical laws of our kingdom of England."

Now, the ecclesiastical laws of the kingdom of England made no provisions for the consecration of Romish or dissenting churches or chapels; and when the charter speaks of churches and chapels to arise within the Maryland colony which are to be consecrated "according to the ecclesiastical laws of the kingdom of England," it is speaking in the sense of English law, and plainly means such churches and chapels as were provided for by the laws of the kingdom. We must not imagine so absurd a thing, as that the King of England would grant to a subject a charter investing him with the right to set up, in a distant province of the empire, a hostile religion, with exclusive power, whose very existence and worship were forbidden by the laws of England. The presentation to the churches of the Province was in the Proprietor; but with the restriction that every church within the province, if consecrated at all, was consecrated by the Bishop of London or his Commissary, according to the laws of the English Church.

The tenth section of the charter provides and commands that the Province of Maryland, while given to Lord Baltimore, with unusually large and full proprietary rights, shall yet be ever regarded as a part of the empire, owing allegiance to and under its protection. We quote in full the explicit language of this section:

"We will also, out of our abundant grace, for us, our heirs and successors, do firmly charge, constitute, ordain and command, that the said province be of our allegiance; and that all and singular the subjects and liege-men of us, our heirs and successors, transplanted or hereafter to be transplanted, into the province aforesaid, and the children of them, and of others their descendants, whether already born there or hereafter to be born, be and shall be liege-men of us, our heirs and successors of our Kingdom of England and Ireland; and in all things shall be held, treated, reputed and esteemed as the faithful liege-men of us, and our heirs and successors, born within our Kingdom of England; also lands, tenements, revenues, services, and other hereditaments whatsoever, within our Kingdom of England, and other our dominions, to inherit, or otherwise purchase, receive, take, have, hold, buy and possess, and the same to use and enjoy, and the same to give, sell, alien and bequeath; and likewise all privileges, franchises, and liberties of this our Kingdom of England, freely, quietly, and peaceably to have and possess, and the same may use and enjoy in the same manner as our liege-men born, or to be born, within our said Kingdom of England, without impediment, molestation, vexation, impeachment, or grievance of us, or any of our heirs or successors; any statute, ordinance, or provision to the contrary thereof, notwithstanding."

The "privileges," "franchises" and "liberties" of Englishmen were just such as the law gave them, no more, and no less. These "franchises" were ecclesiastical as well as civil, the former defined by the ecclesiastical laws of the kingdom, as were the civil rights of Englishmen by their civil laws. They were to be the same in the Province as in England. Even had the King designed to give special privileges and powers to Lord Baltimore, in favor of the Roman Catholics of the Province, and to the limitation of the "privileges" and "liberties" of the Protestant members of the English Church, such design was rendered null and void by the very language of the charter. For this tenth section says: All privileges, franchises and liberties were to be the same in the Province as to those subjects of the Crown in England, "*any statute, act, ordinance, or provision to the contrary thereof notwithstanding.*"

The seventh section gives to Lord Baltimore very large powers of making and administering laws in and for the Province, but at the close of the section throws a restriction around his power, in these respects, which limits it within the constitution and laws of the kingdom of England. This limitation is expressed in the words —

"so nevertheless that the laws aforesaid be consonant to reason, and be not repugnant or contrary, but (so far as reasonably may be) agreeable to the laws, statutes, customs and rights of this our Kingdom of England."

There is one more clause of the charter to which we would call attention as sustaining all we have said respecting its meaning. The government of Charles the First was perhaps as thoroughly personal as a constitutional government could be. He loved his favorites, and stuck to them, even to desperate extremities; and Lord Baltimore stood high in the personal affection of Charles. That affection influenced the King in the grant of a charter, whose requirements, *under* the English law, Lord Baltimore, as a conscientious Roman Catholic, could never fully carry out. Henrietta Maria, the daughter of the King of France and wife of King Charles, was a Roman Catholic, and Lord Baltimore was a convert to that faith. These intimate relations blinded the judgment of the King, as to the full extent of the difficulty and contradiction which the grant of such a charter to such a man involved. To the mind of the King, who, with all his imperfections of character, was loyal at heart to the Reformed Church of England; in the sense of the English law, the "true Christian religion" was that of the State and Church of England. In the mind and heart of Lord Baltimore, none but the Roman faith and obedience met that description.

The last clause of the charter reveals both the warm personal affection of the King for Lord Baltimore, and, at the same time, his loyalty of heart to the faith and church of England. It seems indeed to imply an impression on the King's mind of future misunderstanding, as to the full meaning of the charter; affecting Lord Baltimore's interest on the one side, and the integrity of the Church in the colony on the other. The last clause of the charter looks to both these, and gives the King's mind in respect to both. We give what is relative to the matter in full:

"And if, peradventure, hereafter it may happen, that any doubts or questions should arise concerning the true sense and meaning of any word, clause or sentence contained in this our present Charter, we will charge and command that interpretation to be applied always and in all things, and in all our courts and judicatories whatsoever, to obtain which shall be judged to be the more beneficial, profitable and favorable to the aforesaid now Baron of Baltimore, his heirs and assigns; *provided always*, that no interpretation thereof be made whereby God's Holy and True Religion, or the allegiance due to us, or our heirs or successors, may in any wise suffer by change, diminution or prejudice."

The affection of Charles for Lord Baltimore prompted the grant of the charter; his foresight of the possible attempt to build up a religion different and hostile to that of the nation, prompted this clause of that charter. The clause was well put in, when we remember that in the Papal judgment all religion outside of the Roman creed is heresy; and all kings who do not obey the Pope are liable to be excommunicated and deposed.

I think that I have now shown quite conclusively, from the state of the English nation, its laws relative to the Roman religion, and finally from the charter itself, that King Charles I. had no power or intention of conferring upon Lord Baltimore the prerogative to establish the Roman Catholic, and exclude or limit the reformed, religion from the Maryland colony. The claim, therefore, made for him is false, as a point of history; and of no value to the cause in whose behalf it is paraded. I shall now attempt to show that all the circumstances in our early colonial history are *against* the assertion of Roman Catholic ascendancy in the colony, and that with such ascendancy, Lord Baltimore and a Roman Catholic Legislature granted toleration and equality to all Christians.

I said before that there is just enough of the semblance of truth in the fiction of Maryland's Catholicity, to mislead the popular mind. But, in reality, Maryland never was a Catholic colony. Her earliest settlement was Protestant, and at no period of her history were the majority of her people of the Roman faith. I make this statement deliberately, and rest for its proofs on the facts of the case. Bozman and Hazzard both tell us that the earliest settlement within the present territory of Maryland was made on Kent Island, in the years 1628 or '29, five or six years before Lord Baltimore's colony touched these shores. William Claiborne of Virginia obtained license from King Charles to explore the waters of the Chesapeake bay, and to establish posts for trading with the Indians anywhere within the bounds of the Virginia charter. Both Chalmers and McMahon testify to this point. The charter of Virginia embraced all the territory two hundred miles north and south of Old Point Comfort along the coast, including all the States of Maryland, Delaware, and one-third of New Jersey, and a good slice of Pennsylvania (Hazzard, vol. i. p. 73). In that colony the Church of England was established by law. A few words from the official documents of the times will show the policy of the English Government relative to matters of religion in her colonies. In the "articles, orders and instructions" for the Virginia colony, issued November 20, 1606, occur these words:

"We do specially ordain, charge and require the presidents and councils (of the two Virginia Colonies) respectively within their several limits and precincts, that they, with all care, diligence and respect, do provide that the true Word and Service of God and Christian faith be preached, and planted, and used," &c.

What that true Word and Service of God — in the eye of the English law—was, is still more apparent in the words, "*according to the doctrine*, rites and religion now professed and established within our realm of England" (1 Henning, 69).

From this colony of Virginia came William Claiborne, a man closely identified with the early history of Maryland. It has been the style of such as have written in the interest of the Catholic toleration theory, to abuse Claiborne, as an unprincipled disturber of the peace of the infant colony, and as a rebel against the rightful authority of Lord Baltimore. In explanation of his relation to the Maryland colony, and to show what manner of man Claiborne was, in the estimation of his king, and of the loyal Governors of Virginia, we will present a few facts from the records of the times. From the time of the first issue of the Virginia charter to the year 1624, the affairs of the colony were managed by the company from London; but then the charter was annulled by the King, and twelve persons were appointed to reside in the colony, and manage its affairs (1 Hazzard, 191-192). William Claiborne was one of the twelve. King James I. of England died in the year 1625, and was succeeded in the throne by his son Charles I. In the same year King Charles commissioned Sir George Yeardley, one of the Council, Governor, and William Claiborne, Secretary of State, of and for the colony and plantation of Virginia. The words of the commission say:

"Forasmuch as the affairs of state in said colony and plantation may necessarily require some person of quality and trust to be employed as Secretary, . . . our will and pleasure is, and we do by these presents nominate and assign you, the said Wm. Claiborne, to be our Secretary of State . . ."

The ground of this appointment, as alleged in the King's commission, was the *quality* and *trustworthiness* of the man (1 Hazzard, 233). When Gov. Yeardley died and Harvey succeeded, Claiborne continued Secretary of State — McMahon says, "abundantly evidencing the high estimation in which he was then held." We make these quotations to show Claiborne's character and explain his future action. While Secretary of State for Virginia, Claiborne received from the Governors of Virginia — McMahon says "from the English government"— licenses to *discover* and establish in the Chesapeake Bay, and within the territory of Virginia, trading-posts from which he might carry on commerce with the Indians. From a petition made by him to King Charles in the year 1638 we learn that —

"he discovered, and did then plant upon an Island in the great Bay of Chesapeake, in Virginia, and by them named Kent Island, which they bought of the kings of the country, and built houses, transported cattle and settled people thereon, to their very great cost and charges" (2 Bozman, 582).

The exact year of this settlement is not here stated, but in "Breviat of the proceedings of the Lord Baltimore" it is stated —

"that the Island called Kent was seated and peopled under the Virginian government, three or four years before the King's grant to him" (1 Hazzard, 628).

Baltimore's grant was made in 1632. Three or four years carry us back to 1628 or '9. William Claiborne in a lawful way discovered and purchased Kent Island, and took up the lands according to the custom of the colony at that time (Streeter's *Maryland Two Hundred Years Ago*). To show how completely organized was the settlement, we have the fact that burgesses from there sat in the Assembly of Virginia.

The Virginia records show that there were, at first, about one hundred settlers under Claiborne on Kent Island. Their founder provided for their spiritual wants in the presence and ministration of the Rev. Richard James of the English Church. Surely in all this William Claiborne was acting in a very manly and honest way. But his rights on Kent Island have yet a firmer basis. In the year 1630, influenced perhaps by the knowledge that Lord Baltimore was about to apply for a grant of the Virginia lands, Claiborne applied to King Charles, and received from him a license still more explicit, and one which justified him in regarding that part of the territory as permanently secured to himself and his settlers. This license is dated May 16, 1631, and runs thus:—

"These are to license and authorize you, the said William Claiborne, one of the Council, and the Secretary of the State, for our Colony of Virginia, his associates and company, freely and without molestation, from time to time to trade for corn, furs, &c., with their ships, boats, men and merchandise, in all seas, coasts, harbors, lands or territories in or near those parts of America for which there is not already a patent granted to others for *sole trade;* giving and by these presents granting unto the said William Claiborne full power to *direct* and *govern*, correct and punish such of our subjects as may or shall be under his command in his voyages and discoveries" (1 Bozman, 266, Note).

Rev. Ethan Allen, D. D., to whom we are greatly indebted for help in this paper, says in "Sketches on the Early History of Maryland to the year 1650":

"From the mere wording of the King's license to Claiborne, it may not appear from first sight to have had any reference to Kent Island; but in his petition to the King, and the Council's decision thereon in 1639, that it was so understood. And it was supposed by Claiborne, and the King also, to give him, that is Claiborne, the authority to govern the discoveries he might make. The title to territory, according to usage, was to be derived from the colonial authorities, but here the power to exercise government was given him."

We now come to the time when Lord Baltimore enters into our history. He was a native of Yorkshire, England, and represented

## MARYLAND NEVER A ROMAN CATHOLIC COLONY.

that county in Parliament. His education was first at [
College, Oxford, and afterward on the Continent. Robert
Lord Treasurer, made George Calvert his Secretary; fro
office he was advanced to be Clerk of the Council. He was kr
by King James in 1618, and in 1619 became one of the two
taries of State. While in this office the King gave him a pa
proprietor of the whole south-eastern peninsula of New Foun
to which Calvert gave the name of Avalon, the ancient n
Glastonbury, the seat of the renowned Abbey, which was re
by tradition, to have been the tomb of Joseph of Arimathe
first preached the Gospel there and founded a church. Tr
said that a "miraculous thorn" which flowered on Christm
was the veritable staff with which Joseph aided his steps fro
Holy Land to Avalon. Calvert gave the name of Avalon
settlement in New Foundland. An able historian says:

"This dependence upon a tradition which rests upon the very weakest a
may be regarded as a token of Calvert's mind at that period, to receive with
faith those questionable narratives, which Fuller justly describes as 'bein
puffed up with the leaven of monkery'" (Anderson's Colonial Church Histo
p. 404).

George Calvert was full of zeal, and sought, as An
testifies —

"and his efforts to make the Avalon of the New World a precious seec
Christianity to its benighted inhabitants, were as great as if the dark legend l
a true record of Holy Writ."

To this time he had seemed to be a loyal member of the chu
his baptism; but in the year 1624 he announced to King Jame
he had entered the Roman Church, and resigned his of
Secretary of State, saying that he could no longer hold it
safe conscience, (Fuller's Worthies, Yorkshire, pp. 201,
But Calvert stood high in the esteem and affection of King
who, like his son Charles, held fast to his personal favorites
when doing so offended the people, and trenched upon his f
to the laws of the realm. He retained Calvert as a member
Privy Council, and created him Lord Baltimore, of Baltim
Ireland, by which title he is afterwards known in history.
quent events seemed to discourage him in the direction
Avalon colony, and he withdrew from it entirely. But he d

renounce his intention to found a colony in the New World. Casting his eye further south, he saw the fair and broad domain covered by the Virginia charter, and sought to obtain part of this territory for himself. In the year 1629 we find Lord Baltimore at Jamestown, in Virginia. The Royal instructions to the colonial authorities required all who came into the colony to take the oath of *allegiance*, and that of *supremacy*, to the King of England. Baltimore declined to take these oaths; and after sailing up the Chesapeake to examine it, returned to England, where Streeter says he was the next January, 1630. At the English Court he used his influence to obtain a part of the Virginia territory, and finally procured from Charles the promise of such grant. But the first Lord Baltimore died before the charter was executed; and the grant was made out to his son, Cecilius Calvert, the Second Lord Baltimore, on the 16th of June, 1632.

The charter included about eight millions of acres of land, embracing the peninsula between the Chesapeake and Delaware Bays, on the Eastern Shore, all the Western Shore of the present territory of Maryland, and northward to the fortieth degree of latitude, a little north of Philadelphia. The ground of action influencing the King and his Council in this invasion of territory, which was within the original Virginia charter, is probably that suggested by Bozman, viz. that as the whole Province was now governed by the King, as a part of the empire, and this large section of it was yet *unsettled* and *uncultivated*, it was just and wise to adopt a policy which would sooner fill it with a civilized and Christian people. Nor would we say that this view of it was wrong, so long as it did not contravene rights which the King had already granted; but there was a positive injustice and wrong in such contravention, which King Charles never designed, and which his subsequent utterances show that he regarded with strong disapprobation. The King called the new colony Maryland, in honor of his Queen Henrietta Maria, and describes it as " an *uncultivated* country in the parts of America, and partly occupied by savages." King Charles might readily have fallen into this mistake, and also his Council, being far from the country, and unacquainted with its geography. But Lord Baltimore knew it was not true. Within this territory there were two Christian settlements — a Protestant colony of Swedes on the western shore of the Delaware river, and the Kent Island settlement under

Claiborne. Of this latter Lord Baltimore was fully acquainted, and he could not, in truth, say that it was "*unsettled* and *uncultivated.*" In his petition to the King in 1638, Claiborne says:

"Lord Baltimore took notice of it when there" (2 Bozman, 582).

A pamphlet published in England in the year 1655 says —

"that Lord Baltimore pretended, though not truly, that the country was unplanted, and that his suggestions to the King that those parts were uncultivated and unplanted, except by a barbarous people, not having the knowledge of God, was a misinformation."

This is quite a gentle term of condemnation for an act which led to the breaking up of a peaceful community, and to the shedding of human blood. True, the settlement on Kent Island was small; one hundred Christian settlers only; but one hundred was a larger proportion to the territory of Kent Island than Baltimore's two hundred to the territory of the whole State. As late as 1648 the whole population of Baltimore's colony did not exceed four hundred, including the Kent Island settlement. If some interested Puritan, in high favor with Cromwell, had represented the large tract of territory embraced within Lord Baltimore's charter as "*unplanted,*" and asked for all the Eastern or Western Shore, on that ground, or for a new grant of the whole territory, Baltimore and his adherents would have thought themselves greatly misrepresented and wronged. Yet there would have been as much truth in such a representation, and as much justice in such a grant, as there were in Baltimore's representation to King Charles and the grounds upon which he sought his charter. Indeed, knowing as he did of Claiborne's settlement under the King's license, Baltimore's action in the premises looks very much like a sharp turn of a shrewd politician to do Claiborne out of his rights. I shall have more to say upon this point, showing that as his charter was made to include Kent Island by misrepresentation, so his possession of it came by violence and injustice.

I think I have made good my point that the earliest settlement of Maryland was not Roman Catholic; but in bringing out and sustaining our main position, that the act of the Maryland Legislature in 1649 was not a free act of a Roman Catholic Governor and Legislature, an act of grace to Protestants, and for the extension of religious liberty, it will be needful for us to go more fully into the facts of the times.

Lord Baltimore's charter, dated June 1632, immediately called out a protest from the Virginia colony. Both Hazzard and Bozman tell us that the result of this appeal left Lord Baltimore in the possession of his charter, and referred the Virginia colony to the English courts to adjudicate any interests which were compromised. The matter was heard in the Court of the Star Chamber, to whom the King referred the petition of the Virginia colony, on the 25th of June, in the year 1633. Both parties were to set down in writing their propositions and answers to be presented to the court. These requirements were complied with, and in July—

"their lordships having heard and maturely considered the said propositions, answers and reasons, and whatsoever else was urged on either side, did think fit to leave Lord Baltimore to his patent, and the other parties to the course of the law according to their desire. But for the preventing of further questions and differences, their lordships did think and order *that things stand as they do*—the planters on either side shall have free traffic and commerce with each other, &c."

Such is the reading of the decision according to Hazzard. The same was in the first edition of Bozman, but in his second edition he follows Chalmers, and reads for "that things stand as they do," *that things standing as they do*. The true sense of the decision is, that things were to remain as they were, until decided by a due course of law; that is, the Virginia planters were not to be deprived of Kent Island, nor was Lord Baltimore's patent to be vacated. The prior claim of the Virginia planters was to be left, as they desired, to the law to decide for or against them. The Star Chamber did not decide against either. So the Virginians understood the decision, and Burk, the Virginia historian, says (2 Burk, 39)—

"the Board acknowledged the justice of the claim of the Virginia planters." "They certainly left the matter open for the decision of the law courts as these planters desired."

Lord Baltimore's colony left England in the fall of 1633, and arrived in Maryland the next spring, under the supervision of his brother Leonard Calvert as Lieutenant-Governor. Old England was good enough for Lord Baltimore. Romanists tell us that Maryland was to be a haven of refuge for their persecuted people; but Lord Baltimore, a young man in the vigor of twenty-eight years, preferred Old England to the discomforts of Maryland and the dangers of the sea. An able writer says:

## MARYLAND NEVER A ROMAN CATHOLIC COLONY.

"It must not be overlooked that the first and second Lords Baltimore were very different men. The elder was perhaps influenced by religious considerations in founding the Maryland colony; the younger, as proof in abundance shows, had his eye upon the pecuniary advantages to be derived from his large grant of land, in no small degree" (Ethan Allen's American Ecclesiastical History).

The colonists spent part of the winter of 1633-34 in the West Indies, and on their way north touched at Jamestown, the Virginia settlement. They were hospitably entertained for a few days as the guests of the Virginians. William Claiborne was there, a citizen of Virginia, a member of the Governor's Council and Secretary of State. Governor Calvert at once claimed him as a member of the Maryland plantation, and demanded that he relinquish all relation to and dependence on Virginia. Claiborne resisted this claim, and denied Lord Baltimore's right to Kent Island; but he appealed to the Governor and Council of Virginia for advice how to act in the case. Surely this does not look like self-will and lawlessness on the part of Claiborne. Dr. Allen remarks:

"The claim of Governor Calvert was not only that the Kent Island settlers, with their Proprietor, should submit to his government, but it involved their title to the right of soil also. Admit Governor Calvert's claim, which, as we have seen, the Star Chamber did not decide upon, but referred to the courts of law, and it involved the necessity of abandoning their plantations, and thus losing the fruits of past years of labor, or of a repurchase of the soil from Lord Baltimore, upon his own terms of plantation, as they were called, so that instead of holding under Captain Claiborne, upon the annual payment of two capons, Lord Baltimore would become entitled to his quit rents from them."

In response to Claiborne's request for advice from the Governor and Council, it was answered by the Board that —

"they wondered why any such question was made; that they knew no reason why they should render up the rights of the place of the Island of Kent more than any other formerly given to this the Virginia colony by his Majesty's patent, and that the right of my Lord Baltimore's grant being yet undetermined in England, we are bound in duty and by our oaths to maintain the rights and privileges of this colony," &c. (2 Bozman, 571).

Very clearly indeed does this show that the authorities did not understand the matter as settled by the decision of the Star Chamber, but only as referring the opposing claims to the courts for decision, until which time each party was to remain in the quiet enjoyment of what they had. They therefore felt and determined it to be their duty to maintain the rights of the Kent Islanders until such decision was reached. They would not relinquish their rights, nor allow Claiborne to yield his proprietorship. That they were right in their judgment and action is evident from what took place in England, only three or four months later. On the 22d of July the same year the committee of the Privy Council for the colonies, known as the Commissioners for Plantations, write to the Governor and Council of Virginia in these words:

"His Majesty doth let you know that 'tis not intended that interests which have been settled when you were a corporation should be impeached; that for the present, they may enjoy their estates with the same freedom and privilege as they did before the recalling of their patents; to which purpose we do also authorize you to dispose of such portions of land to all those planters, being freemen, as you had power to do before the year 1625" (1 Hazzard, 345; 2 Bozman, 42, note; 2 Bozman, 571).

This language shows beyond question that those private rights which were settled on Kent Island, were never intended to be invaded or unsettled by Lord Baltimore's charter. Was it strange that Claiborne and others interested on Kent Island, should suppose from this assurance of the commissioners that their interests were not to be impeached by Lord Baltimore's patent? Can any man wonder that, with the support of the Governor and Council of Virginia, with the judgment of the King's Privy Council, and with the favorable letters of the Commissioners of Plantations, Captain Claiborne declined compliance with Lord Baltimore's demands?

If any one were disposed to question the conclusion we reach, there is one more fragment of evidence on the point which ought to be sufficiently conclusive. Claiborne made a petition to the King after he had been dispossessed by force of arms, in which he alludes to a letter which had been written by his Majesty on the matter. He says:

"His Majesty was pleased to signify his royal pleasure by letter, intimating that it was contrary to justice and to the true intent of his Majesty's grant to Lord Baltimore to dispossess them of Kent Island; that notwithstanding the said patent, the petitioners should have freedom of trade, requiring the Governor and all others in Virginia to be aiding and assisting them, prohibiting the Lord Baltimore and all pretenders (under) him to offer them any violence, or to disturb or molest them in their Kent Island plantation."

Bozman says —

"It is not to be doubted that a letter of this import was signed by his Majesty" (2 Bozman, 69, note).

Let us follow the facts, and see how they bear upon the much lauded justice and generosity of Lord Baltimore. In the face of Claiborne's occupancy under a royal license, and despite the instructions of his King as to the true intent of his charter, Lord Baltimore, by violence and force of arms, drove Claiborne out of his Kent Island possessions. True, an attempt was made to give a greater color of justice to these violent proceedings, on the ground that Claiborne was stirring up the Indians to hostility against the St. Mary's settlement of Lord Baltimore. Streeter says, "This charge was shown to be false by the testimony of the chief of the Patuxents," (Streeter's Papers relating to the early history of Maryland, 6, Note). Father White, the Jesuit annalist of the colony, lays the blame at the door of a certain Captain Fleet, who was under Claiborne's influence. Fleet was a Protestant, and an Indian trader, from Virginia. Our readers may judge for themselves how much credence is to be attached to this assertion, and how far it was believed at St. Mary's, when we tell them that Fleet resided in the Maryland colony, that the Governor and Council gave him four thousand acres of land, accepted him as a member of the Legislature, and appointed him to head an expedition against the Indians. Some excuse was needed to give color to the wrong contemplated against Claiborne and his Protestant colony, and this seemed most feasible. Bozman—misled, mainly, it would seem, by Chalmers—countenances this reflection upon Claiborne. Streeter says of the charge against Claiborne, made by Father White, and emphasized by the action of the Maryland authorities against him:

"It is difficult to reconcile this assertion with the known position of Fleete in the Colony for several years afterward, and with facts which, instead of countenancing such a view, prove Fleete to have been in opposition to Claiborne, and to have been the means of throwing an unfounded imputation upon him, of having attempted to excite the savages to acts of hostility against the Marylanders" (Streeter's Maryland Papers, p. 68).

Mr. Streeter's allusion to Fleet's "known position" refers to offices of trust and confidence which he held under the Lord Baltimore government, a position utterly inconsistent with the assertion of Father White, that he, "seduced by Claiborne, stirred up the minds of the natives against us." The further observations of Mr. Streeter go far to clear Claiborne of the imputation, and convict Fleet of falsehood and duplicity. He says:

"The insinuations and hints of Capt. Fleete turned the suspicions of the colonists against Claiborne; and measures were immediately adopted for holding a conference with the king of the Patuxents and other chiefs to investigate the matter. The meeting was held on the 20th of June, 1634, and there were present four of the principal members of the Virginia colony; George Calvert and Frederick Winter and some others on the part of the Marylanders, and Capt. Claiborne in person. Capt. Fleete did not appear. After the interpreters were sworn, the chief of the Patuxents was informed that they had come to inquire respecting a statement of Capt. Fleete to the Governor of Maryland, and the lives of some of their people depended on his testimony. He answered their interrogatories, and in the course of his replies denied that Capt. Claiborne had ever spoken against the Marylanders, or attempted to induce him to attack or injure them. The other chiefs gave a similar testimony. The chief further asserted that in an interview at St. Mary's, Fleete had asked him whether Capt. Claiborne had not spoken with him against the colony, and he had told him that nothing of the kind had occurred. He therefore indignantly declared that Fleete was a liar, and if he were present he would tell him so to his face. Further, upon his, that is the chief, expressing surprise that they should place any confidence in such a man as Fleete, the Virginia Commissioners replied that 'the gentlemen of Yawacomaco did not know Capt. Fleete as well as they of Virginia, because they were late come.'"

Another Indian testified to Fleet's efforts to awaken suspicions and excite hostilities between the colonists of St. Mary's and Kent Island. Fleet was an able, but in all probability an unprincipled man. Governor Calvert had no right to trust in him, but he availed himself of his abilities, and was closely associated with him in many ways. It is worthy of remark that this point of the testimony of the Patuxent chief which Streeter gives so fully in favor of Claiborne, is made by Chalmers against him, and also that Lord Baltimore's order to "seize and punish him" was on the pretext that he stirred up the Indians against the Maryland colony.

Bozman, misled by Chalmers, has fallen into the same error, and maintains the charge against Claiborne which the Indians had set aside. In spite of all this testimony, the Maryland authorities proceeded to enforce their will against Claiborne and the Kent Island settlers, without awaiting that due course of law by which the King and Star Chamber had determined the questions at issue were to be adjusted. Gradually the two communities drifted into open hostilities, boats were armed and sent out, and men were killed on both sides. The wrong was clearly on the side of Lord Baltimore. The question had not yet been adjudicated in the courts; and, until such was the case, Claiborne was justified in forcible resistance. An armed expedition in 1637 reduced Kent Island to subjection, and brought back some prisoners to St. Mary's. Thomas Smith, an officer with a commission from Claiborne, underwent the farce of a trial, and was condemned and hanged for piracy and murder. The execution of this poor man was clearly a judicial murder, if ever one was perpetrated under the forms of law. He was indicted for felony and piracy, when, under a commission, he was only obeying the officer his king had put over him. The armed expedition of Leonard Calvert succeeded in robbing Claiborne and others of their rights. The records of the Virginia colony show that among other sufferers was the Rev. Mr. James, the pastor of the Kent Island settlement. Leaving the colony, he went to England with Claiborne, and his goods were confiscated by the Government of St. Mary's.

I have one more fact germane to this point; it is the estimate put upon all these proceedings in England when intelligence of them came there. William Claiborne repaired to England, and appeared before his king, expelled from his rights, and attainted by the act of Baltimore's Legislature, of murder and piracy. He appeared before King Charles, the superior lord of both these men, who had given Claiborne his *license* and Baltimore his *patent*. The King surely knew the meaning and intent of both, and was prepared to estimate impartially the conduct of each toward the other. What was the King's judgment? Did he approve Lord Baltimore's violent course, and condemn Claiborne as a pirate and murderer? The King issued this order to Lord Baltimore, which I shall give in full :

" Whereas, formerly by our Royal letters to the Governor and Council of Virginia, and to our other officers and subjects in those parts, we signified our pleasure that William Claiborne, David Morehead, and other planters in the Island near Virginia which they have nominated Kent Island, *should in no sort be interrupted in their trade or plantation by you, or any other on your right, but rather be encouraged to proceed in so good a work*, we do now understand that, though your agents had notice of our said pleasure, signified by our letters, yet contrary thereto they have slain three of our subjects there, and by force possessed themselves of that Island, and carried away both the estates of said planters. Now, out of our Royal care to prevent such disorders, as we have referred to our Commissioners of Plantations the examination of the truth of these complaints, and require them to proceed therein according to justice, so, now, by these particular letters to yourself, we strictly *require and command you* to perform what our general letter did enjoin, and that the above named planters and their agents may enjoy in the meantime their possessions and be safe in their persons and goods there, without disturbance or farther trouble by *you or any of yours, until that case be decided*. And herein we expect your ready conformity, that there be no cause of any further mistake. Dated July 14, 1638."

This letter is clear and explicit, and no amount of sophistical comment can change its sense, upon certain points. It makes the original intention of the King clear beyond question, that the rights of trade and plantation already vested on the Kent Island, under the King's license and the Virginia charter, were not to be disturbed by Baltimore's patent. This order brings out more clearly what the King meant in a former letter, when he said, "it was contrary to justice, and to the true intent of the grant to Lord Baltimore, to dispossess them of Kent Island." In this order he says, "Lord Baltimore's agents had by force possessed themselves of the Island." Surely if, in the King's intention, it belonged to Baltimore, he would not speak of his taking possession of his own as a wrong done by him. But the King does so speak, and commands Lord Baltimore to make restitution to the wronged planters, until the issue was decided by law. We think we can see clearly the point of difficulty, and the seeming contradiction in the words of the King, and the final decision of the Commissioners of Plantations, in favor of Lord Baltimore. Lord Baltimore had represented to the King the whole country as "*unsettled and uncultivated except by savages.*" On this representation the King issued to Lord Baltimore his patent, excluding in intention every idea of its interference with rights already vested by a previous license to William Claiborne. As soon as the King found that the patent did geographically include Kent Island, every utterance of his shows that his intention, rather than the geographical limits of the charter, was the rule by which he interpreted it. Baltimore stuck to the literal geographical limit of the charter, gotten from the King by misrepresentation; and pushed, to the last degree, the advantage which it gave him. The King felt the wrong of depriving men of rights which preceded those of Baltimore, and in all his utterances on the subject to them, and to Lord Baltimore, showed his sense of that wrong. The matter in dispute was ultimately decided by the "Commissioners of Plantations" against William Claiborne; but long before such decision was given, Lord Baltimore had shown his determination to push his claim to the uttermost, and, right or wrong, to get all he could from his charter. The decision was finally in his favor; probably because they looked at the simple letter of the charter; and as Kent Island was geographically comprehended in it by the letter of the law, they gave it to Lord Baltimore, and confirmed him in it. But even in that decision they left Claiborne to the ordinary courts of justice for pecuniary reparation from the wrong of which he complained.

We shall see, before we close, that the end was not yet, and that Lord Baltimore had to reap the fruits of his own sowing, in a harvest of disquietude and loss. He subdued Kent Island, confiscated the estates of some of the more prominent persons, among others of the Rev. Mr. James, their English clergyman, even seizing by a legal writ from St. Mary's, the cattle of his widow after her husband's death in England. Having finished his work of conquest, Baltimore appointed George Evelyn and John Longford, both Roman Catholics, the former Commander, the other High Sheriff of Kent Island, and thus reduced an independent Protestant community, whose existence dated some years before his charter, to alien and hostile control.

The work of spoliation was now complete. The King's overweening affection and confidence towards Lord Baltimore bound him to the legal construction of a charter which made him an unwilling party in a great wrong. That wrong he could not then well amend, by recasting the charter of Maryland. But the King of England did make amends, as far as in him lay, to William Claiborne for the wrong he had unwittingly done him. In the year 1642, after the King had time for a deliberate review of all the facts in the case, and for a calm apprehension of his great wrong to a faithful subject, he appointed William Claiborne King's Treasurer for life in the colony of Virginia. The appointment was directly from the King (1 Hazzard 493). Just ten days before Claiborne received this appointment of honor and emolument from his King, Lord Baltimore was summoned before the House of Lords on charges for some offence, we know not now of what character, but at least so grave that he was put under bonds not to leave the kingdom (Streeter, pp. 29, 30). Surely there is an aspect of retributive justice in the attitude of these two men at this time. Claiborne came over to America after the question of his proprietary rights to Kent Island was decided against him, and in the year 1640, received from the Governor and Council of Virginia a large grant of land, for great services rendered that colony. The relations of the two colonies were so amicable at that time, and the courtesies between the two Governors, Wyatt and Calvert, such, that Claiborne was encouraged to seek for the recovery of his private property on Kent Island. His agent on Kent Island, Mr. George Scovell, applied to the Governor and Council for the recovery of such property; he received a reply, dated August 21, 1640; and was told that all property in the hands of Claiborne at the time of his withdrawal was forfeited to the Lord Proprietor, and that he stood attainted for piracy and murder. It is said that Lord Baltimore did not accept the acts of this Legislature, because they rejected the laws which he sent them from England to enact, and insisted on originating laws of their own. This is very probable, for it was not until the next year, 1639, that the Lord Proprietor assented to their originating legislation of their own, subject, however, to his approval or veto. Streeter says:

"If, as is asserted, Lord Baltimore never assented to the acts of the Assembly of 1638, and if, as is undeniable, that assent was necessary to the legality of those acts, it would be difficult to show on what grounds the authorities of Maryland could have based their claim to hold his property."

This was the last blow, the last attempt of the Maryland authorities to insult the man they had so foully wronged. This same year he received the grants of land from Virginia in honor and reward of distinguished services, and in due time his king wiped off from his name and reputation the imputation of pirate and murderer, and compensated his losses by the honorable and lucrative office of King's Treasurer for life in Virginia. At the same time, or ten days before, Lord Baltimore stands under charges before the House of Lords, and is bonded not to leave the kingdom. I think this array of facts will go very far to dissipate the oft-vaunted assertion of the justice and generosity of the administration of Lord Baltimore. They do settle beyond question the fact that the first settlement of Maryland was Protestant, and that the attitude of Lord Baltimore to that *older* colony was one of *unscrupulous and unrelenting hostility*.

To determine intelligently the influences which shaped the religious and ecclesiastical policy of the Maryland colony, we must consider the nationality and religious composition of the colonists. The school-books—at least too many of them—and certain partisan newspapers, tell us that they were Irish and Catholic. We presume the ground for this inference is that, as Lord Baltimore was a Romanist, he brought principally Roman Catholic emigrants.

Why not, by the same logic, infer that, as he was an Englishman, he brought English colonists? The fact is, they were a very mixed people. After the two hundred who came in with Leonard Calvert, the later accessions were mostly from Virginia, and the larger proportion of all the emigrants Englishmen; but among them were Germans, French, Hollanders, Spaniards, Italians, and some Irish. Father White, the Jesuit annalist of the colony, tells us that the number who left England with Leonard Calvert was two hundred, of whom seventeen were gentlemen; the rest were servants, mechanics, laborers and dependents of various kinds. The reverend annalist does not tell us how many were Roman Catholics or how many were Protestants, but he gives us the basis of an inference that the larger portion were Protestants, at the very foundation of the colony. The good father tells us —

"that at the Christmas festival on their way out from England, which they celebrated in the West Indies, that the day might be more joyfully celebrated the wine flowed freely, and some who drank immoderately, about thirty of the number, were seized with fever the next day, and twelve of them died, two being Catholics — Nicholas Fairfax and James Barefoot."

If the other ten who died, being Protestants, indicate, even approximately, the proportion of Protestants in the expedition, it becomes at once evidence that the great proportion of Baltimore's settlers were not Roman Catholics. Possibly the seventeen gentlemen were mostly Romanists—personal friends of Lord Baltimore—but the stronger probability is, that the large majority of the others were not. The colonists arrived in Maryland on the 27th of March, 1634, and bought from the Indians 150,000 acres of land for a few hatchets, axes, hoes and yards of cloth — pretty much the same policy as that which has prevailed ever since in dealing with these simple children of nature. Within this purchase they founded St. Mary's City, the capital of the province until the year 1694, when it was removed to Annapolis.

To the presumption, justified by the statement of Father White, that the majority of the settlers were Protestants, we are to add many facts and circumstances going to prove most conclusively that Maryland was never properly a Roman Catholic colony. One thing is certain: Lord Baltimore designed, if possible, to make it such, and did all in his power and consistent with his pecuniary interest to further that end. He brought two Jesuit priests to minister to the small number of his own faith ; but, as far as all the records we possess enable us to judge, no spiritual provision whatever was made for the majority, or the large minority of the Protestant settlers. We cannot tell the exact date when the first English clergyman came into the colony. The records show a Protestant chapel in 1638, and in 1642, eight years from the settlement, three Protestant churches of the English faith appear — Trinity, St. George's, and one in St. Clement's Hundred of which we do not know the name. To this date none of the authorities speak of a second Roman chapel, while there are at least three Protestant churches ; and to our day Protestant Episcopal churches stand on or near these sites. This fact shows the majority of Protestants, as the increase of their churches was a sure index of the numbers and needs.

In the year 1644, William Claiborne, heading a military expedition, regained possession of Kent Island, where he was welcomed by the people, who were glad to be rid of the Roman Catholic officers, whom, against their assent, and as one of the fruits of their conquest, Governor Calvert had put over them. Calvert made an expedition to Kent to displace Claiborne, but was unsuccessful (2 Bozman, 287-290).

The next year Ingle's rebellion drove Governor Calvert out of the colony. It is said that he acted under a commission from the Parliament, which was then entirely under the control of the Puritans. About this time, or a little before, Parliament made the Earl of Warwick "Governor-in-Chief, and Lord High Admiral of all the American colonies, with a Council of five Peers and twelve Commoners to assist him." They also declared any one who took part with the King, in the civil war then raging in England between King and Parliament, as liable to confiscation and sequestration (2 Bozman, 289). It did certainly look as if the Parliament intended to govern the colonies directly from England. This fact is still more significant when we remember, as Streeter says, Lord Baltimore was, in 1642, under bonds not to leave the kingdom. Under all the circumstances of the case, there need be little question that Ingle had the *secret*, if not the open countenance of the Puritan authorities in England. Ingle's occupancy of St. Mary's continued about two years, and was, no doubt, a crucial time to the Roman Catholic friends of Lord Baltimore. The Jesuit Missions were broken up, and the Fathers sent to England for trial (Streeter, 33-34). Father White says of these events—

"that there were certain soldiers, unjust, plunderers, Englishmen indeed by birth, of the heterodox faith"—

—of course orthodox Romanists never invade anybody's possessions, nor appropriate other people's rights—

—"had invaded with arms almost the entire colony; had plundered, burnt, and finally, having abducted the priests and driven the Governor himself into exile, had reduced it to a miserable servitude."

No doubt these were stormy times for the St. Mary's people, and especially for Lord Baltimore's friends; but he and they might have remembered that they were not guiltless in this matter; and that some of the people of Maryland, especially those of Kent Island, perhaps had a lively recollection of the expulsion of their proprietor, the confiscations, the imprisonments and executions done by Leonard Calvert and his associates, before the voice of the English law courts had decided in his favor and against Claiborne's claim. It has ever been claimed, as the exclusive prerogative of Baltimore's co-religionists, to persecute and oppress; and none cry louder, or complain more bitterly, when the chalice of their own poisoning is commended to their lips.

Governor Calvert returned to his government at the close of the year 1646. Aided by troops from Virginia, he recovered Kent Island in the beginning of the next year, and died June the 9th, aged 40 years, after having named Thomas Green to succeed him. The affairs of the colony were now in the most dilapidated state. Population had declined to 150 on Kent Island, and 250 at St. Mary's. The colony was evidently in danger of extinction, or if not that, of being taken out of the hands of Lord Baltimore. The Parliament—or rather Cromwell and his army—were now masters in England. The King was seized by Cromwell, June 3, 1647, and murdered January 30, 1649, putting the most extreme and radical Puritan element in the entire control of the British Empire throughout the world. The colony was a very difficult and complex thing for Lord Baltimore to manage under such circumstances — decline in the colony itself, threatening its extinction; at home, the complete ascendancy of an irresponsible Puritan despotism. To save the colony from ruin, he must settle its government; to save it to himself, he must conciliate the Puritan masters at home. What did he do to attain these results? He appointed Robert Vaughn, a Protestant, Commander of Kent Island, and Colonel William Stone, a Protestant, and the most energetic man in the colony, to be his Governor of the province of Maryland. This appointment was made in the year 1648, while the King lay in prison. The ends and aims which determined it are beyond question. It was a politic stroke of self protection on the part of Lord Baltimore; no more, no less. The appointment was made August 17th, 1648, on the condition, as his commission says, that he was to bring in five hundred settlers. The commission phrases it thus: "In some sort to procure five hundred people, of British or Irish descent, to come from other places, and plant and reside within the province of Maryland." Of Stone, John Langford, formerly Lord Baltimore's High Sheriff, says in a pamphlet published in London in the year 1655:

"he was well known to be a zealous and well affected Protestant; he was generally known to have been always zealously affected to the Parliament."

These five hundred must, in the very nature of the case, have been mainly Protestant. Stone, who had been High Sheriff of Northampton County, Virginia, brought his five hundred settlers from that colony, where all were Protestants, and from henceforth the immense majority of the colony were to be Protestants, and all its future legislation be in their hands. Whatever legislation they might determine on religion, would possibly be in the direction of the anti-Roman Catholic legislation of the home government. Lord Baltimore saw this, and, so far as in him lay, he would provide against it. He therefore appointed Stone, an energetic man and Protestant, his Governor, to repair his wasting colony, and to control the turbulent elements of a rather radical and revolutionary Protestantism, into whose hands his colony was just passing.

The oath administered by Lord Baltimore to Col. Stone is of special interest in its religious features. It runs thus:

"I will not by myself, nor any person, directly or indirectly trouble, molest or discountenance any person in that province professing to believe in Jesus Christ, and in particular no Roman Catholic, for, or in respect to his or her religion, nor in his or her free exercise thereof within said province, so that they be not unfaithful to his said Lordship, or molest or conspire against the civil government established here.

under him. Nor will I make any difference of persons in conferring rewards, offices, or favors proceeding from the authority which his Lordship hath conferred upon me, as his lieutenant here, for or in respect to their said religion respectively, but merely as I shall find them faithful and well deserving to his Lordship, and, to the best of my understanding, endowed with moral virtues and abilities, fitting for such rewards, offices, and favors, wherein my prime aim and end from time to time shall be the advancement of his said Lordship's service here, and the public unity and good of the province, without any partiality to any or another *sinister end whatever;* and if any other officer or person whatsoever shall, during the time of my being his Lordship's lieutenant, without my consent or privity, molest or disturb any person within his province professing to believe in Jesus Christ, merely for, or in respect to his or her free religion, or free exercise thereof, upon notice or complaint made to me, I will apply my power and authority to relieve and to protect any person so molested or troubled, whereby he may have right done him from any damage which he shall suffer in that kind, and to the utmost of my power will cause all and every such person or persons, as shall molest or trouble any other person or persons in that manner, to be punished."

This oath has been lauded beyond measure, as the very concentration of justice and generosity, and as showing the highest breadth of mind, the largest liberality of heart. But calm and impartial historical justice requires us to analyze the facts, and refute the errors concerning it. Chalmers, who has misled many persons concerning the history of Maryland, gives this oath in a most inaccurate and deceptive way. I will give his version of the clause in full, that the reader may compare them. Chalmers' version runs thus:

"I will not by myself, nor any person, directly or indirectly trouble, molest, or discountenance any person professing to believe in Jesus Christ, for or in respect to religion. Nor will I make any difference of persons in conferring rewards, offices or favors, for or in respect to religion, but merely as I shall find them faithful and well-deserving, endowed with moral virtues and abilities. My aim shall be public unity, and if any other officer or person molest any person professing to believe in Jesus Christ, in respect of his religion, I will protect any person so molested, and will —— any person as shall molest any other person to be punished."

The most important clause of the oath, and of the deepest historic significance, couched in the words "*and in particular no Roman Catholic,*" is left out altogether by *Chalmers*. But this is not the worst deception of Chalmers' version of the matter. He represents this as the oath taken by the Governor and Council, between the years 1637 and 1657. This statement gives the impression that this oath was first taken in 1637, and always afterwards when such oaths were administered, until 1657. True, this oath was administered between these years, but never until 1648, never until the

Protestant Stone was made Governor, Protestant Councillors and a Protestant Secretary of State filled the offices and administered the affairs of the colony, and a Protestant population and Legislature were about to shape the future legislation of the colony.

Leonard Calvert became the Governor of the colony in 1634. Dr. Allen says, "History records no oath of office which he took, until the one ordered by the Maryland Assembly of 1638, which is this":

"I do swear, that while I am a member of this province, I will bear true faith to the Right Honorable Cecilius, Lord Proprietary of this province, and his heirs — saving my allegiance to the Crown of England — and the said province and him and them, and his and their due rights and jurisdictions, and all and every of them will aid, defend and maintain to the utmost of my power, the peace and welfare of the people I will ever procure, as far as I may, and to none will I delay or deny right, but equal justice will administer in all things, to my best skill, according to the laws of this province, so help me God."

This oath Governor Calvert took March 20, 1638. There is no trace of any other. During his absence in England in 1643 and 1644, Mr. Brent acted as temporary Governor. The oath which he took may be found in 2 Bozman 254. It is in substance the same as that above to Calvert, but nothing like that of Stone. The previous oaths were imposed by the Maryland Assembly. The oath of Stone was imposed by Lord Baltimore himself. Dr. Allen says:

"Now then, does this oath propose toleration as now understood to all religious sects and denominations of Christians, conscientiously differing from each other? No such thing is specified. The word toleration is not in it, but *protect* is in it. The Governor is made to swear, 'I will apply my power and authority to relieve and protect any person so molested.' Protection was the idea of that day, not toleration: that was of after growth. Nor was it the object of the oath to grant toleration."

Yielding to the force of circumstances, the complete ascendancy of the English Parliament, the danger of losing his colonial government, if not possessions, and considering the large proportion of Protestants in his province, Lord Baltimore found it advisable to appoint a Protestant Governor, a Protestant Secretary of State, and one-half of the other members of the Council, Protestants. And what clearly is the main object of this oath to be taken by this Protestant Governor? Not simply to protect Episcopalians, Presbyterians and Puritans. For the two latter the government at home would certainly see to, and the officers now appointed also. It was that this Governor should not molest, trouble or discountenance any person whatsoever, in the said province, professing to believe in Jesus Christ, *in particular no Roman Catholic;* the very thing Chalmers *left out.*

A contemporary and friend of Lord Baltimore, Langford, already quoted, says, in his pamphlet of 1655, that —

"Lord Baltimore appointed this oath to be taken by the aforesaid officers, when he made Captain Stone, Governor; Mr. Thomas Hatton, Secretary; and others of his Council there; who, being of a different judgment in religion from himself, his Lordship thought it but reasonable and fit, that as he did oblige the Governor by oath not to disturb any there who did believe in Jesus Christ, so to express the Roman Catholics in particular, who were of his own judgment in matters of religion."

Beyond all question, the oath was imposed to protect Roman Catholics, and not to give toleration to Protestants. It was a wise and good thing, but was never done before, and was now done under the pressure of necessity and for self-preservation. It was extorted, and not a free act of grace and favor to others. It was an unavoidable necessity of Lord Baltimore's position, when struggling against difficulties endangering the loss of all his interest in the Maryland colony.

The Legislature met the next year, 1649, the first under Governor Stone's administration. This Assembly passed the famous "Act concerning Religion." There has been much false statement concerning the origin and meaning of this piece of legislation, and a great deal of eulogium upon the Roman Catholic Proprietor and Legislature for such a wise and generous policy. We have already seen that Lord Baltimore was in a position compelling him to appoint a Protestant Governor, Secretary of State and majority of the Council, and that the oath to Colonel Stone, which appears so broad and liberal to all Christians, was to insure protection to Roman Catholics from molestation on the score of their religion. The state of things which made that oath a necessity of his position continued and was intensified. The Protestant population of the colony was already in the ascendant; the Puritan government of Cromwell had the mastery of all England. Influenced by all these considerations, the Lord Proprietor would gladly suggest of himself such legislation, or accept it when enacted, as looked to the results contemplated by the appointment of Stone, and his oath of office. There has been much discussion about the complexion of the Legislature, whether the majority of its members were Roman Catholic or Protestant. Bozman says: "There are strong grounds to believe that the majority were Protestants, if not Protestants of the Puritanic order." We know that the Governor, Secretary of State and the majority of the Council were Protestants. Bozman adds —

"There are strong reasons for supposing that the majority of the burgesses were Protestants, as they certainly were the next year, 1650."

There is other testimony, from contemporary sources, friendly to Lord Baltimore, which would seem to be quite explicit. The Maryland Assembly of the year 1648 wrote a letter to Lord Baltimore, describing the depressed and wretched condition of the colony as it emerged from the Ingle rebellion, at the return of Governor Calvert from Virginia. They say:

"Most of your Lordship's friends here were despoiled of their whole estate, and sent away as banished persons out of the province. Those few that remained were plundered."

They also add, that the first Assembly after Governor Calvert's return —

"two or three only excepted, it consisted of that rebelled party, and Governor Calvert's professed enemies."

To this Protestant ascendancy, already established, is added, two years later, five hundred Puritan Protestants, and we see at once that the colony is Protestant beyond question. Thus the boasted "Act of Toleration" proves to have been the result of Protestant influence, and *most likely* an act of Protestant legislation, and altogether necessary to the maintenance of Lord Baltimore's position and rights as proprietor of the colony.

The remarks of Bozman, as to this piece of legislation, are very just. Alluding to Chalmers' statement on the subject, that this Legislature was composed chiefly of Roman Catholics, Bozman says:

"The error (as it appears to me) of a learned annalist, when he says, in his encomium of this act, that this Assembly of 1649 was 'composed chiefly of Roman Catholics,' has propagated the opinion, generally adopted, that this act of religious toleration proceeded from a Roman Catholic government. An opinion certainly incorrect, as to those who now administered the Maryland government, since unquestionably the Governor and most of the Council were Protestants, (of the old Church of England perhaps,) and in all probability a majority of the Assembly were so, with a few Puritans mixed up with them. The act of Assembly may be said, indeed, to have been the political measure of a Roman Catholic nobleman, and so far the Roman Catholics are entitled to all the credit which may accrue to them from this measure of an individual of their sect."

He adds:

"But without the slightest endeavor to detract from the personal merit of Cecilius Calvert, Lord Baltimore, it may be safely maintained, that the history of affairs throughout the British Empire in Europe, at this time, clearly demonstrates that this measure of general religious toleration, now adopted by his Lordship, flowed rather from a prudent policy, than any personal disposition to a general religious toleration."

This supposition is confirmed by the fact that no word or act of Lord Baltimore, during the earlier years of his proprietorship, looked in that direction. Bozman says further:

"The Government of Virginia was now also ferreting out from their hiding-places all the Puritans who lurked in that ancient dominion. Maryland, unfortunately for his Lordship, became an asylum for most of them. The inhabitants of this province now formed a heterodox mixture of almost every Christian sect. To keep peace among them, a general toleration was obviously the only prudential measure to be adopted."

To confirm this judgment of Bozman, we need but look at the terms of the 3d Section of the Article on Religion:

"Whosoever shall, in a reproachful way, call any one an Heretic, Schismatic, Idolater, Puritan, Presbyterian, Independent, Popish Priest, Jesuit, Jesuited Papist, Lutheran, Anabaptist, Brownist, Antinomian, Barrowist, Roundhead, Separatist, or any other name or term, shall forfeit £10 sterling, or if not able, shall be publicly whipped and imprisoned till the party offended be satisfied, by the offender asking forgiveness publicly."

These terms all show the presence and temper of a preponderating Puritanism.

We need not now follow the development of the colony farther. We have reached the point in its history in which this vital question inheres. New emigrants came, and the country grew. New counties were formed and new settlements made; but the Protestant population was always many times more than the Roman Catholic. The Roman Catholic historian, McSherry, says that —

"at this time, and even forty-three years later, the Roman Catholics were the majority in Maryland."

Against this we have only to put Lord Baltimore's own testimony. In 1676 he was before the Court of Privy Council, and made a statement in writing, still extant, that —

"the population of the colony was 20,000, of whom three-fourths were Presbyterians, Independents and Quakers" (2 Anderson, 613).

In 1686, what is known in history as the Protestant Revolution displaced Lord Baltimore from his proprietary rights; and in the year 1692, the population then being 25,000, the Assembly of Maryland passed an act making the Church of England the established church. This fact shows that the Church of England had the majority over all in the Legislature. This continued to be the religious status of the colony, under the law, until the time of the Revolution. In 1697 a report was made by the county sheriffs to the Governor, by order, of the state of religion, the number of churches and ministers in each county. The report of the Governor to the Bishop of London, as made up from these items, is still extant in the archives of Maryland, and in those of the Bishop, and shows nine teachers and ministers of the Roman Catholic, Presbyterian and Quakers, and twenty places of worship, not of the Church of England, while that church had eighteen ministers and twenty-five places of worship.

But we will close. Much more testimony might be adduced, all concurring with what we have brought forward. More is not needed to prove that Maryland was never Catholic Maryland, in the sense that is claimed for her — perverted school histories, and interested politicians, to the contrary notwithstanding. The documents quoted cover one hundred and thirty years — documents never impeached, never contradicted, all telling the same story.

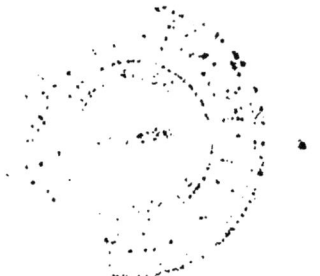

Printed by Libri Plureos GmbH in Hamburg, Germany